On the Job:
Readings about Work for English Language Learners

Wendi K. Halstead

All people and businesses referred to in this textbook are fictional. Any similarities to actual individuals, living or dead, or to business establishments are completely coincidental.

© 2008 by Wendi K. Halstead. All rights reserved.
ISBN 978-0-6151-9591-9

Table of Contents

Unit 1: Safety Is Everybody's Responsibility ………………………… p. 1

Unit 2: Running a Restaurant……………………………………...…… p. 11

Unit 3: Teachers ……………………………….... ……………………… p. 21

Unit 4: Health Insurance Benefits ……………….. …………………... p. 31

Unit 5: Hiring the Disabled Can Be a Good Deal for Employers… p. 41

Unit 6: Retirement Benefits ……………………... …………………… p. 51

Unit 7: Who Will Take Care of the Children?………………………... p. 61

Word Search

Directions: Find the words.

C	O	M	P	E	N	S	A	T	I	O	N	R	E	S
Q	D	E	R	E	P	E	T	I	T	I	V	E	T	A
X	J	D	O	C	A	R	E	F	U	L	N	S	B	F
Z	S	I	T	E	S	H	A	Z	A	R	D	P	Y	E
I	I	C	E	P	S	X	A	D	R	P	M	O	Z	T
R	V	A	C	W	E	E	M	E	R	G	E	N	C	Y
K	S	L	T	B	N	W	A	Z	R	R	I	S	K	J
W	I	L	W	P	G	F	Q	T	S	Q	T	I	I	K
L	S	H	A	R	E	Y	U	V	D	S	V	B	W	C
U	D	U	W	O	R	K	P	L	A	C	E	L	F	C
G	J	K	V	V	C	E	Q	U	I	P	M	E	N	T
Y	V	E	H	I	C	L	E	C	D	S	A	J	T	P
F	F	U	N	D	A	N	G	E	R	B	L	L	F	W
W	K	J	Z	E	K	C	A	B	L	D	S	T	B	N

careful
compensation
danger
emergency
equipment
fund

hazard
medical
passenger
protect
provide
repetitive

responsible
risk
safety
share
site
vehicle
workplace

Lesson 1

Prereading Discussion Questions:

Have you ever been hurt at work? If so, what happened?

What kinds of accidents can happen at work?

Who is responsible for the accident?
Who is responsible for the medical bills?

Summary:

Everyone, employers and workers alike, is responsible for job safety. The employer needs to provide training in how to do the job safely, and employees are responsible for listening to instructions and following directions. Workers must also use the safety equipment as required.

---

share = use equally
provide = give
sites = locations
equipment = things that are necessary to do an activity
dangers = risks; what can hurt you

repetitive = repeating
vehicle = car, bus, truck, SUV, van, etc.
passengers = riders
hazards = dangers; risks
compensation = payment
fund = collection of money

Job Safety is Everybody's Business[*]

[1] Some jobs are dangerous and it is essential that workers are safe at work. Both employers and employees share the responsibility to make sure that everyone is protected.

[2] One way for employees to be safe is to use equipment which protects them from the dangers on the job. At some work sites, the employer provides safety equipment, but at other jobs, the worker must buy the necessary safety equipment.

[3] There are many types of protective equipment that will keep workers safe on the job. On noisy work sites, employees need to wear earplugs to protect their hearing. On jobs that use chemicals, workers need to wear masks or respirators that protect their lungs. If a job requires heavy lifting or repetitive actions, workers may need to wear a supportive device, like a back brace or a knee or wrist support.

[4] Some jobs require workers to drive cars, trucks, or other vehicles. Employees who must drive should be safe. They need to always wear seat belts, and make sure that any passengers wear them, too. It's also important for the workers not to drive too fast. It can also be unsafe if they are very tired when they drive.

[5] Employers can do a lot to make the workplace safer. They can provide their workers with protective equipment. They also need to train them to use the equipment safely and what to do in an emergency. They can also rotate jobs to prevent repetitive stress injuries.

[6] Workers have responsibilities, too. They need to follow all safety rules and instructions. They need to use safety equipment and protective clothing when needed. They need to keep work areas clean and neat and look out for their co-workers. They need to know what to do in an emergency and report any hazards to their employer.

[7] Even though the workers and the company are careful, sometimes workers get hurt on the job. If they do, their medical care is paid for by a worker's compensation fund. It is something like insurance for the company. The company pays money every month, and if a worker gets hurt, the fund pays for the worker's medical care.

*Adapted from http://www.cdc.gov/niosh/adoldoc.html; http://www.cdc.gov/niosh/motralrt.html 6/27/07

Vocabulary in Context

Directions: Find the synonyms in the reading.

Line #	Find a synonym for:	Synonym
1	not safe	
2	very important	
4	something you have a duty to do; something you must do	
8	things that are required for an activity	
10	locations	
17	loud; with a lot of noise	
29	motorized transportation	
35	fatigued	
38	place of employment	
42	very serious situation	
43	change regularly	
52	people who work together	
54	dangers; risks	
57	cautious	
64	employee	

Comprehension Check

Directions: Read each sentence and decide if it is <u>true</u> or <u>false</u>.

1. Everybody is responsible for job safety.
2. Employers always provide safety equipment.
3. Some workers need to use masks or respirators to protect their lungs.
4. Trucks don't have seat belts.
5. Repetitive stress injuries happen from doing the same task over and over again.
6. Workers must pay for their own medical care if they are hurt on the job.

Directions: Answer these questions:

7. What are some things that employees can do to be safe on the job?
8. Who provides safety equipment?
9. What are some examples of safety equipment?
10. Why is it important for worker to wear earplugs? In what situations are they necessary? Give examples.
11. What can employers do to make sure that the employees are safe at work?
12. Why are motor vehicles dangerous at work? What can employees do to make sure they are safer? What can employers do?
13. What are some responsibilities that workers have?
14. Who pays for medical care when an employee is hurt?

In other words...

Directions: Match the sentences with the same meanings.

___1. Some jobs are dangerous.

___2. It is essential that workers are safe at work.

___3. At some work sites, the employer provides safety equipment.

___4. At other jobs, the worker must buy the necessary safety equipment.

___5. In noisy work sites, employees need to wear ear plugs to protect their hearing.

___6. Employees who must drive should be safe.

___7. They need to always wear seat belts, and make sure that any passengers wear them, too.

___8. Employers need to train workers to use the equipment safely.

___9. They need to know what to do in an emergency.

___10. If a worker gets hurt, their medical care is paid for by a worker's compensation fund.

a) The driver is responsible for wearing a seat belt and for making sure that any riders wear one, too.

b) On other job sites, the employees must buy their own safety equipment.

c) Workers need to wear protection for their ears if the workplace is loud.

d) It is extremely important for workers to be safe on the job.

e) Medical care for injured workers is paid for by worker's compensation.

f) There are some occupations which are risky.

g) Knowing what to do in an emergency is very important.

h) Good driving is essential for workers who operate motor vehicles.

i) It is the responsibility of employers to make sure their employees know how to use equipment in a safe manner.

j) In some workplaces, the company buys protective equipment for the workers to use.

Main Ideas

Directions: Refer to the reading to find the main ideas of these paragraphs:

Paragraph 3
    a) Respirators protect workers' lungs from chemicals.
    b) Workers must provide their own safety equipment.
    c) Protective equipment can prevent injuries on the job.

Paragraph 5
    a) Employers need to do all they can to make the workplace safe for their workers.
    b) Employers must pay for safety equipment.
    c) Workers need to use respirators.

Paragraph 6
    a) Workers must keep their work area clean.
    b) Employees are also responsible for work safety.
    c) Workers must tell the boss if something isn't safe.

Paragraph 7
    a) Workers compensation is an insurance policy.
    b) Worker's compensation will pay for medical care if a worker gets hurt.
    c) Workers get hurt every day.

Synonyms

Directions: Match the words with the same meanings.

___1. tired   a. required

___2. passengers   b. fatigued

___3. employees   c. locations

___4. necessary   d. directions

___5. protected   e. not messy

___6. sites   f. dangers

___7. instructions   g. riders

___8. neat   h. rapidly

___9. hazards   i. kept safe

___10. fast   j. workers

Suffix –ive

The suffixe -ive means *having a particular quality.* The new word is an adjective.

From the reading:

Other examples:

Example	Meaning
repetitive	with repetition
protective	with protection
descriptive	with description
creative	with creativity
active	with activity
corrective	with correction
destructive	with destruction
expensive	with expense

Directions: Use the examples to complete the sentences. Be sure to use a plural form when necessary. Use each word only once.

1. New cars are very _____ so most people don't buy them very often.
2. My job is very _____. I do the same thing all day long.
3. Susan is very tired today. Her nephew is a very _____ child and she babysat for him all day.
4. Hurricane Katrina was a very _____ storm.
5. It is important to use _____ equipment if you have a dangerous job.
6. Mark wrote a very _____ story about his trip to the mountains.
7. I don't see very well, so I need _____ lenses to drive.
8. Children are very _____. I love to watch them draw pictures.

Scanning

What Hazards Should I Watch Out For?*

Type of Work	Hazards (Problems)	Solutions
Janitor/ Maintenance	• Toxic Chemicals in cleaning products • Blood on discarded needles	• Masks and respirators • Training
Food Service	• Slippery Floors • Hot Cooking Equipment • Sharp Objects	• Good shoes • Protective equipment • Training
Retail/Sales	• Violent Crimes • Heavy lifting	• Protective equipment • Training
Office/Clerical	• Stress • Harassment • Poor computer work station design	• Protective equipment • techniques for reducing stress • sensitivity training
Manufacturing	• Cuts • Head injuries • Machine related dangers	• Protective equipment • Training

Directions: Scan the table to find the answers to the questions.

1. What types of problems can maintenance workers have? What are some solutions to these problems? Are all maintenance workers exposed to the same risks?

2. What kind of worker is in danger from slippery floors? Why do you think that's true? What other types of dangers are there for these workers?

3. For what kind of workers is poor computer station design a risk? What can be done to help them?

4. Who is at risk for head injuries and cuts? What is another problem for this type of worker?

5. What are some of the dangers for people who work in stores?

6. Why is training a solution to safety problems?

---

* Adapted from http://www.cdc.gov/niosh/adoldoc.html , 6/27/07

Crossword Puzzle

ACROSS
1. keep safe
8. riders
10. place of employment
11. very important
14. risks; what can hurt you
15. car, bus, truck, SUV, van, etc.
16. collection of money
17. locations

DOWN
2. fatigued
3. payment
4. repeating; doing something over and over again
5. not safe
6. a very serious situation
7. dangers; risks
9. use equally
11. things that are necessary to do an activity
12. give
13. cautious

✏️ Get ready to write!

Prepare for writing
Directions: **On a separate piece of paper, outline the article.** Use the main ideas you found in the exercise on p.6 as the headings. Next, add the details that go with the main ideas. Your teacher will help you.

Write a summary
Directions: **Use the outline to help you write 4 paragraphs which summarize the article.** Be sure to:
- use a capital letter at the beginning of each sentence.
- use periods to separate sentences.
- indent to show the beginning of each paragraph.

Tip:

When we talk about obligation, we use the following:

Workers <u>must use</u> safety equipment.
Workers <u>have to use</u> safety equipment.
Workers <u>need to use</u> safety equipment.

<u>It is necessary</u> for workers <u>to use</u> safety equipment.
<u>It is essential</u> for workers <u>to use</u> safety equipment.
<u>Using</u> safety equipment <u>is necessary.</u>

Your experience counts!

Directions: Write about or discuss the following questions.
1. Have you ever been hurt on the job? If so, how did it happen? What kind of injury did you have?
2. Did you miss time from work? Did you get paid for the time you missed?
3. What is the situation for injured workers in other countries?

Word Search

Directions: Find the words.

A	D	M	I	N	I	S	T	R	A	T	I	V	E	I
Q	U	A	L	I	F	I	C	A	T	I	O	N	S	N
R	E	S	P	O	N	S	I	B	I	L	I	T	Y	S
C	O	M	M	U	N	I	C	A	T	I	O	N	S	U
P	R	E	P	A	R	A	T	I	O	N	M	U	U	R
R	E	S	T	A	U	R	A	N	T	T	A	T	P	A
O	G	P	P	S	V	I	V	E	E	E	N	R	P	N
M	U	E	O	S	A	V	A	M	M	R	A	I	L	C
O	L	C	S	I	H	A	C	O	P	N	G	T	I	E
T	A	I	I	S	D	Z	A	N	L	H	E	I	E	W
I	T	A	T	T	E	N	T	I	O	N	R	O	S	P
O	I	L	I	A	T	Q	I	T	Y	O	W	N	E	R
N	O	L	O	N	A	Q	O	O	E	N	E	R	G	Y
P	N	Y	N	T	I	T	N	R	E	X	U	E	H	C
Z	S	I	S	I	L	L	N	E	S	S	Q	P	J	F

administrative
assistant
attention
communication
detail
employees
energy
especially

illness
insurance
intern
manager
monitor
nutrition
owner
positions

preparation
promotion
qualifications
regulations
responsibility
restaurant
supplies
vacation

Lesson 2

Prereading Discussion Questions:

What are some restaurant jobs?
What qualifications do you need to get these jobs?
What do you have to do to keep these jobs?

Have you ever worked in a restaurant?
Is restaurant work a good job? Why or why not?

Summary:

Every restaurant needs to have a manager. In a small restaurant, the manager may be the owner, but in a large restaurant, there maybe one manager and several assistant managers.

Restaurant managers have positions with a lot of responsibility. They have to coordinate the work of all the employees, so they can work as a team. Managers have to make sure that the restaurant follows all health laws, and they must supervise all employees. They also have to order food and other supplies.

There is more than one way to become the manager of the restaurant. Some people take courses at a 2-year or 4-year college to learn about running a restaurant in a classroom. On the other hand, sometimes good employees are promoted to manager from lower level positions in the restaurant.

---

to supervise = to manage

owner = proprietor

positions = jobs

coordinate = organize; direct

team = people who work together, like in sports

supplies = necessities; things which are needed

to run a restaurant = to operate a restaurant

promoted = he/she got a better job in the same company

Running a Restaurant

[1] Every restaurant must have one person in charge, to supervise everything which happens in the restaurant. This person is the manager. If the restaurant is big, there may be one or more assistants to help. The assistants are often responsible for different shifts if the restaurant is open twenty-four hours a day.

[2] On average, restaurant managers make around $30,000 per year. In big companies and restaurants, the managers and other employees may get benefits, too. This is particularly true if the restaurant is part of a large chain. Medical and dental insurance are examples of benefits. Other examples are retirement benefits and time off with pay for vacation, holidays, and illness.

[3] Managers may work very long hours, especially if they own the restaurant. Many work fifty to sixty hours a week. Because the owners are self-employed, they do not get overtime pay.

[4] Restaurant managers have many different responsibilities. They have to pay attention to administrative tasks that make the restaurant run well. They order food and other supplies for the restaurant. They need to schedule the workers. The manager also has to hire new workers. They train and supervise the restaurant employees, too.

[5] Managers do other things as well. They need to monitor the work of the employees to be sure that all health regulations and liquor licensing laws are obeyed. In addition, they have to arrange for the repair of equipment when it breaks down.

[6] Many restaurant chains hire managers with 2-year or 4-year degrees in hospitality management. In these programs, students learn about nutrition and food preparation. The students also take classes in accounting, business management, and computer science. In addition, they may also work as interns. This means that they work in temporary jobs to practice what they are learning in class. They get these jobs through the school and they may receive academic credit for their work.

[7] Some companies promote good workers to management positions. These workers must have good communication skills and attention to detail. Restaurant managers must also enjoy working with people. In addition, they need to have a lot of energy because they sometimes need to work long shifts.

Vocabulary in Context

Directions: Find the synonyms in the reading.

Line #	Find a synonym for:	Synonym
2	responsible (2 words)	
12	typically; usually; normally (2 words)	
17	something from an employer in addition to money	
17	especially	
19	series; many restaurants with the same name	
29	working for themselves; they own the business	
32	duties; obligations	
33	organizational; directorial	
42	check; observe; supervise	
46	to make plans for (3 words)	
48	stops working (2 words)	
51	programs about hotels and restaurants (2 words)	
53	healthy eating	
58	not permanent	

Comprehension Check

Directions: Read each sentence and decide if it is true or false.

1. In large restaurants, there are often assistant managers.
2. Sometimes restaurant workers get benefits.
3. The waiters and waitresses are responsible for hiring.
4. Managers must be sure all employees follow health and safety laws.
5. There are no laws about getting a liquor license.
6. It isn't necessary for managers to be good with people.
7. Restaurant work pays well.
8. Everyone who works in a restaurant gets benefits.

Directions: Answer these questions:

9. Who is in charge if the restaurant is open around the clock?
10. What is a shift? Typically, how many hours are there in a shift? What is it called if you work longer hours?
11. What are some of the responsibilities of a restaurant manager? Do you think you would like this job?
12. Where do restaurant managers get their training? What do they need to learn?
13. What is an intern? How do they get the position?
14. Why do restaurant managers need to have a lot of energy? Do you think you would be good at it?

In other words...

Directions: Match the sentences with the same meanings.

___1. Every restaurant must have one person in charge, to supervise everything which happens.

___2. The assistants are often responsible for different shifts.

___3. In big companies and restaurants, the managers and other employees may get benefits, too.

___4. This is particularly true if the restaurant is part of a large chain.

___5. Managers may work very long hours, especially if they own the restaurant.

___6. Because they are self-employed, they do not get overtime pay.

___7. Managers need to monitor the work of the employees to be sure that all health regulations and liquor licensing laws are obeyed.

___8. Managers have to arrange for the repair of equipment when it breaks down.

___9. Students may get jobs as interns while they are in school.

___10. These workers must have good communication skills.

a) It is possible that employees of big restaurants and other companies will get benefits as well.

b) Workers who own their own business do not get overtime pay.

c) Managers need to be sure that the restaurant complies with all health and licensing regulations.

d) Frequently, it is the assistant managers who are responsible for different periods of time.

e) In particular, managers who own the restaurant work very long hours.

f) When machines stop working, the manager must call a repair service to fix them.

g) Sometimes students get internships before they graduate so they will have some experience.

h) It is necessary for restaurants to have someone who is responsible for everything that goes on.

i) It is essential that these workers know how to communicate well.

j) This is especially true if the restaurant is part of a company with many locations.

Main Ideas

Directions: Refer to the reading to find the main ideas of these paragraphs:

Paragraph 2
    a) There may be assistants.
    b) Some restaurant managers get both money and benefits.
    c) All restaurant employees get benefits.

Paragraphs 3, 4, and 5
    a) Managers work long hours and have many responsibilities.
    b) It is necessary for managers to hire new employees.
    c) Managers must obey the law.

Paragraphs 6 and 7
    a) There are two ways to become the manager of a restaurant.
    b) Restaurant managers go to school.
    c) If you work hard, you can be a restaurant manager.

Synonyms

Directions: Match the words with the same meanings.

____1. in charge   a. supervisor

____2. manager   b. sickness

____3. particularly   c. healthy eating

____4. illness   d. to get a better job

____5. responsibilities   e. specifics; small things

____6. nutrition   f. responsible for

____7. to get a promotion   g. get

____8. receive   h. vitality

____9. details   i. duties; things which much be done

____10. energy   j. especially

Suffix –er

The suffix –er means *a person who…..*
It is used on the end of a verb. The new word is a noun.

From the reading:

	Example	Meaning
	manager	a person who manages
	worker	a person who works
	owner	a person who owns
	employer	a person who employs; a person (or company) who gives jobs
	teacher	a person who teaches
	writer	a person who writes; author
	dancer	a person who dances
	singer	a person who sings

Other examples:

Directions: Use the examples to complete the sentences. Be sure to use a plural form when necessary. Use each word only once.

1. Restaurant _____ take direction from the manager of the restaurant.

2. _____ have many responsibilities, including scheduling the workers and ordering food and other supplies.

3. _____ sometimes give medical insurance to their workers.

4. My sister is a wonderful _____. She has a lovely voice.

5. I am a home _____. My husband and I bought our house 10 years ago.

6. My English _____ works full-time for the school system.

7. Thomas is an excellent _____. He has published three books.

8. Héctor is an excellent _____. He has a wonderful sense of rhythm.

17

Scanning

Food Safety[*]

Product	Cook until...
Egg and Egg dishes	
Eggs	yolk and white are firm
Egg dishes	160° F.
Ground Meats	
Turkey, Chicken	165° F.
Veal, beef, lamb, pork	160° F.
Fresh Beef	at least 145° F.
Fresh Veal	at least 145° F.
Fresh Lamb	at least 145° F.
Fresh Pork	
Roast	at least 160° F.
Fresh ham (raw)	at least 160° F.
Pre-cooked ham (to reheat)	at least 140° F.
Poultry	
Whole chicken	180°F.
Whole turkey	180°F
Roasted breast	170°F
Roasted thighs & wings	180°F
Stuffing (in the bird or separately)	165°F
Duck and Goose	180°F
Seafood	
Fin Fish	it is opaque and flaky
Shrimp, lobster, crab	it is red and opaque
Scallops	it is milky white and opaque
Clams, mussels, oysters	shells open

Directions: Use the table to answer these questions about how to cook food safely.

1. How do you know if your food has reached the correct temperature?
2. What is the proper temperature for a whole, roasted chicken or turkey?
3. What is stuffing? Traditionally, where is it cooked?
4. Why do the instructions for beef, veal, lamb and pork give a minimum temperature? What happens if you cook it longer? Is it OK to eat it at a lower temperature?
5. What type of seafood should be cooked until it is red and opaque?
6. Is fish ready to eat if it is translucent? What should it look like when it is ready to eat?
7. Why are there two different temperatures for ham?

---

[*] Adapted from http://www.foodsafety.gov/~fsg/fs-cook.html, 9/27/2006

Crossword Puzzle

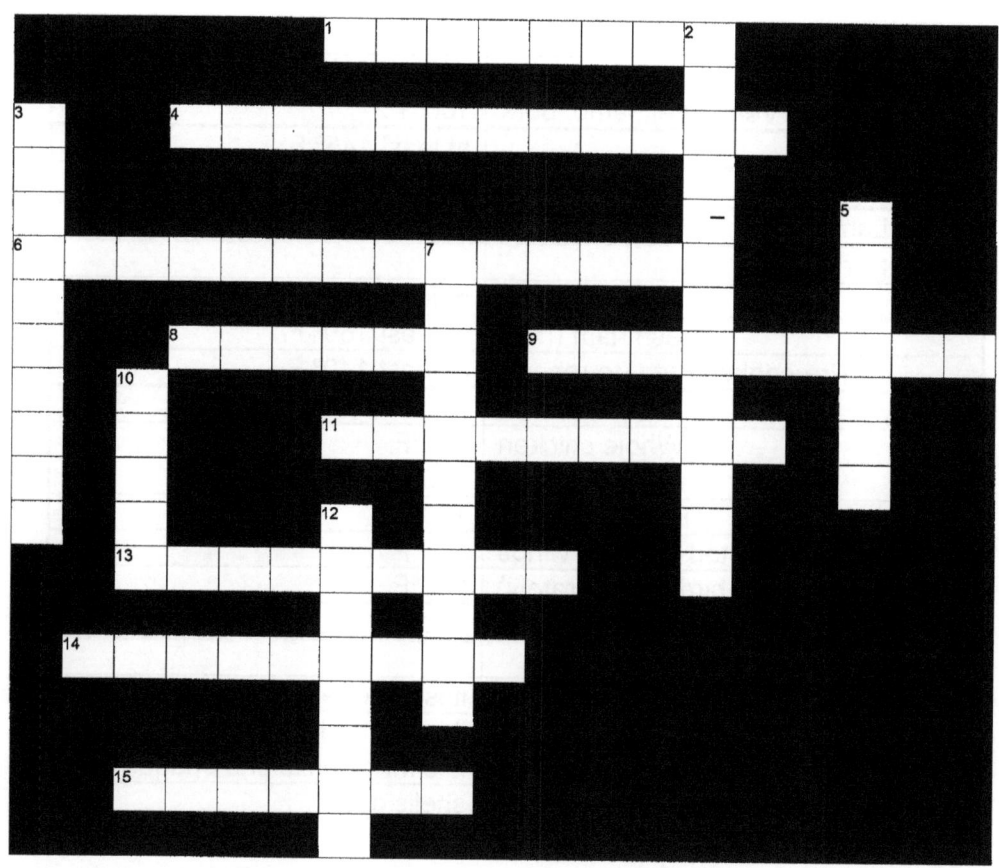

Across
1. something from an employer in addition to money
4. especially
6. organizational; directorial
8. responsibilities
9. not permanent
11. better job in the same company
13. healthy eating
14. usually, normally, on average
15. check; observe

Down
2. working for themselves
3. stops working (2 words)
5. make plans for
7. in charge
10. series; many restaurants with the same name
12. energy

✏️ Get ready to write!

Prepare for writing
Directions: **On a separate piece of paper, outline the article.** Use the main ideas you found in the exercise on p.16 as the headings. Next, add the details that go with the main ideas. Your teacher will help you.

Write a summary
Directions: **Use the outline to help you write 3 paragraphs which summarize the article.** Be sure to:
- use a capital letter at the beginning of each sentence.
- use periods to separate sentences.
- indent to show the beginning of each paragraph.

Tips:
We often want to give examples when we write.
1. When we don't start a new sentence we can use these expressions:
    There is a lot of work that must be done, **like** supervising, ordering supplies, and cleaning.
    There is a lot of work that must be done, **such as** supervising, ordering supplies, and cleaning.
2. When we start a new sentence, we can use these expressions:
    There is a lot of work that must be done. **For example,** the manager must supervise, order supplies, and clean.
    There is a lot of work that must be done. **For instance,** the manager must supervise, order supplies, and clean.

Your experience counts!

Directions: Write about or discuss the following questions.
1. Have you ever worked in a restaurant? If so, did you like it? Why or why not?
2. If you have never done this type of work, do you think you would be interested in it? Why or why not?
3. Compare restaurants in the US with restaurants in other countries. How are they similar? How are they different?
4. Is restaurant work good paying? Does it usually include benefits?
5. Are you good at teamwork? Do you enjoy it or do you prefer to work alone? Is it important to think about what kind of work you prefer when you make decisions about school or work? Why or why not?

Word Search

Directions: Find the words.

I	N	S	T	R	U	C	T	I	O	N	O	I	C	J
D	A	N	G	E	R	O	U	S	D	K	P	Z	U	T
E	N	R	A	C	R	E	A	T	I	V	E	S	R	F
V	W	W	W	P	R	H	S	R	W	M	N	E	R	W
E	U	I	M	P	R	O	V	E	R	T	I	M	E	M
L	S	U	B	J	E	C	T	S	K	P	N	I	N	Y
O	K	V	Z	C	T	X	Q	S	C	Z	G	N	T	J
P	I	L	X	C	I	G	W	F	M	E	S	A	M	F
M	L	M	K	B	R	Q	Z	U	Z	H	H	R	A	C
E	L	Z	T	V	E	L	B	L	A	J	O	S	M	W
N	S	L	O	T	Y	B	D	G	D	D	R	A	M	A
T	D	T	H	O	R	G	P	O	L	I	T	E	F	I
I	M	A	Y	E	H	A	D	G	T	E	A	M	S	A
Z	F	T	R	T	R	A	I	N	I	N	G	T	G	S
X	J	C	O	Z	L	Q	I	V	K	M	E	X	A	M

Creative
Current
Dangerous
Development
Drama
Exam
Improve

Instruction
Openings
Overtime
Polite
Retire
Seminars

Shortage
Skills
Stressful
Subjects
Teams
Training

Lesson 3

Prereading Discussion Questions:

What makes a good teacher?
What makes a bad teacher?

What kind of qualifications does a teacher need to have?

Does the job pay well?
Does it get a lot of respect? Why or why not?

Summary:

Classroom teachers in the United States teach ideas or skills to their students. It's hard work, and many teachers spend extra time working with sports, drama, or music programs. Sometimes they get paid extra for these after school activities and sometimes they don't.

Many people think that teachers have vacation all summer, but for some teachers this isn't true. Many teachers spend their summer taking additional courses in college or teaching summer school.

It is difficult for school districts to find enough qualified teachers. Some people don't want to be teachers because the job can be very stressful. There are also many teachers who will retire in the near future, so that the shortage will continue to be a problem.

---

drama = theater productions
additional = extra
qualified = with the right training or experience
school districts = areas with one school system

stressful = emotionally difficult; with a lot of pressure
retire = stop working; usually because of age
shortage = not enough of something

Teachers*

[1] Do you like working with children? Do you like to work with people from different cultures? Are you organized, dependable, patient, and creative? If so, you might want to be a teacher.

[2] Classroom teachers explain material to their students. Some teachers, like those who teach science or social studies, spend much of their time explaining ideas and facts to their students. Science teachers give instruction on concepts relating to biology or chemistry, and social studies teachers teach things like history and government. Other teachers teach skills, like reading, writing, foreign languages and mathematics.

[3] Younger children get most of their instruction from one teacher, while middle school and high school teachers usually specialize in one or two subjects. The younger children spend their day in just one classroom, but the older kids move from room to room every hour.

[4] Teaching is hard work. Teachers spend a lot of their day preparing lessons, or correcting papers and homework. They have to write tests and sometimes they meet with parents to help children do better in school. Some teachers also help with after-school activities like drama or sports. Many work more than forty hours per week.

[5] Many people think that teachers only have vacation during the summer, but that isn't true for all instructors. Some teach summer school or get another job. Others take classes or go to seminars to learn to be better teachers.

[6] Teachers receive their training at universities and colleges all across the country. College students take classes in how to teach and in child development and psychology. These courses help students pass the licensing exams that they must take to become teachers.

[7] Most teachers earn from $30,000 to $50,000 per year. Teachers usually get more money for more education, so many teachers go back to school for a master's degree. Some teachers also get jobs in the summer, and teachers who coach athletic teams also get extra money.

[8] It is difficult to find enough teachers because teaching can be stressful. Instructors have a lot of work to do, and they sometimes have to manage children who are not well-behaved. Drugs are a problem in some schools, and some schools are dangerous.

[9] There will be many opportunities for educators in the future. There are teacher shortages in a lot of school districts, and many current teachers will retire. This will cause more openings for teachers in the near future.

*Adapted from http://www.bls.gov/k12/help01.htm, 9/21/2006

Vocabulary in Context

Directions: Find the synonyms in the reading.

Line #	Find a synonym for:	Synonym
5	able to think of new ideas	
18	things learned with a lot of practice	
21	teaching	
24	areas of knowledge	
25	use (time)	
35	extra learning experiences (3 words)	
43	classes not more than one or two weeks long	
49	growth; progression	
59	a second college diploma (2 words)	
61	groups of people who play a sport together (2 words)	
65	causing worry	
68	polite	
70	not safe	
73	not enough of something	
75	at this time	
76	empty jobs; positions with no workers	

Comprehension Check

Directions: Read each sentence and decide if it is <u>true</u> or <u>false</u>.

1. Science and Social Studies teachers help their students learn <u>ideas</u>.
2. Reading, Writing, Math, and Foreign Language teachers help students learn to <u>do</u> something.
3. All teachers have vacation in the summer.
4. Teachers with more education earn more money.
5. Some students are rude.
6. In the US, we don't have enough teachers.

Directions: Answer these questions:

7. Do younger children have more than one teacher? Why do you think this is?
8. Why do older children move from one class to another?
9. What are some things which teachers have to do during the school day? What do teachers do after school? What do they do in the summer?
10. Are teachers finished learning when they graduate from college? Is this good or bad? Why?
11. Why are there teacher shortages?
12. What are some of the problems in schools in the US? Can you think of any possible solutions?
13. Do you think you would like to be a teacher? Why or why not?

In other words...

Directions: Match the sentences with the same meanings.

___1. You might want to be a teacher.

___2. Classroom teachers explain concepts to their students.

___3. Middle school and high school teachers usually specialize in one or two subjects.

___4. Younger children spend their day in just one classroom.

___5. Many teachers work more than forty hours a week.

___6. Some teachers also help with after-school activities like drama or sports.

___7. During the summer, some teachers take classes or go to seminars to learn to be better teachers.

___8. Teachers receive their training at universities and colleges all across the country.

___9. There are teacher shortages in many districts.

___10. Retirements will cause more openings for teachers in the near future.

a) Teachers who work with older children usually focus on only one or two subjects.

b) After school activities like drama or sports may take up teachers' time.

c) Colleges and universities nationwide train classroom teachers.

d) Elementary school children don't usually move from one classroom to another.

e) Many school systems do not have enough teachers.

f) There will be many employment opportunities in the field of education because many older teachers will be retiring.

g) Some teachers attend professional development classes and seminars during the summer.

h) Teaching might be a good career choice for you.

i) Teachers work long hours, often more than full-time.

j) Teachers in classrooms give explanations about ideas to their students.

Main Ideas

Directions: Refer to the reading to find the main ideas of these paragraphs:

Paragraph 2
    a) Sometimes teachers explain facts to their students.
    b) Classroom teachers help students understand and use new material.
    c) Sometimes teachers teach skills.

Paragraph 3
    a) Younger children go to elementary school.
    b) Older children go to middle school or high school.
    c) Younger children and older children have different schedules.

Paragraphs 4 and 5
    a) Teachers work harder and longer than most people think.
    b) Teachers just have vacation in the summer
    c) Teachers correct homework.

Paragraphs 8 and 9
    a) Teaching can be stressful.
    b) Many teachers will retire in the near future.
    c) Many school districts are experiencing a shortage of teachers.

Synonyms

Directions: Match the words with the same meanings.

___1. ideas   a. improve

___2. teacher   b. overtime

___3. vacation   c. education

___4. do better   d. polite

___5. drama   e. concepts

___6. more than 40 hours per week   f. free time

___7. training   g. sports

___8. exams   h. instructor

___9. athletic   i. theater

___10. well-behaved   j. tests

Suffix --*ful*

The suffix –*ful* means *with a lot of...*

	Example	Meaning
From the reading:	stressful	with a lot of stress or pressure
Other examples:	beautiful	with a lot of beauty
	harmful	with a lot of harm or damage
	colorful	with a lot of color
	careful	with a lot of care or attention
	helpful	with a lot of help (to give)
	thoughtful	with a lot of thought
	hopeful	with a lot of hope
	painful	with a lot of pain
	useful	with a lot of uses

Directions: Use the examples to complete the sentences. Be sure to use a plural form when necessary. Use each word only once.

1. A bilingual dictionary can be very _____ to ESL students.

2. John knows I like sweets so he brought me cookies. It was a very _____ gift.

3. Children aren't always good, so it can be very _____ to be a parent.

4. The mountains in Colorado are very _____.

5. Smoking cigarettes is _____ to your health.

6. Michael has a lot of car accidents because he is not a _____ driver.

7. It was very _____ when I broke my ankle.

8. Rachel painted the walls red, so the bathroom is very _____.

9. It is difficult to remain _____ when someone you love is sick.

10. Pedro is a very _____ student. He often comes early to class to see if the teacher needs anything.

27

Scanning

Teacher Shortages in Urban School Districts in the United States[*]

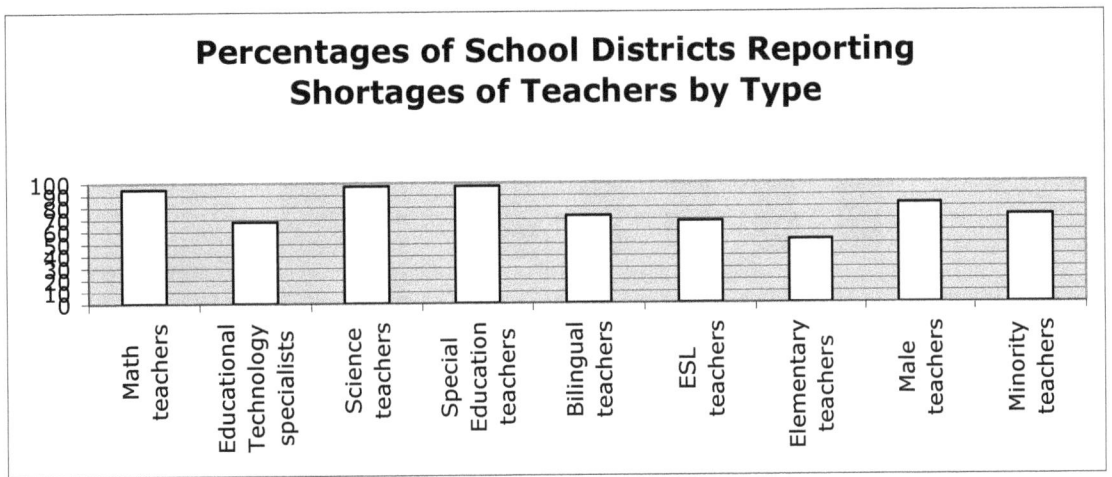

Directions: The above graph represents the results of a poll of school districts in large cities. The survey was done to analyze the types of teacher shortages. Scan the graph to find the answers to these questions.

1. How many categories were analyzed? How many categories represent subject areas? Which areas of specialization are represented on the graph? How many categories represent age groupings of the students? How many categories represent personal characteristics of the teachers?

2. Which three areas have the most critical shortage? Approximately what percentage of school districts said they were experiencing shortages in these categories?

3. Why do you think that these three areas have more of a problem than others?

4. Which category of teacher has the least critical shortage? Why do you think this is the case?

---

[*] based on data from *The Urban Teacher Challenge Report*, Recruiting New Teachers, Inc., http://www.rnt.org, August 18, 2002

Crossword Puzzle

ACROSS
2. do better
5. tests
6. areas of knowledge
9. able to think of new ideas
10. growth; progression
12. short classes
13. well-behaved
14. education
16. at the moment
17. groups of people that play sports together

DOWN
1. more than 40 hours per week
2. teaching
3. jobs with no workers
4. not safe
7. with a lot of pressure or worry
8. theater production
11. not enough of something
12. things learned with a lot of practice
15. stop working, usually because of age

✏️ Get ready to write!

Prepare for writing
Directions: **On a separate piece of paper, outline the article.** Use the main ideas you found in the exercise on p 26. as the headings. Next, add the details that go with the main ideas. Your teacher will help you.

Write a summary
Directions: **Use the outline to help you write 4 paragraphs which summarize the article.** Be sure to:
- use a capital letter at the beginning of each sentence.
- use periods to separate sentences.
- indent to show the beginning of each paragraph.

Tip:
We use the following expressions when we want to show cause and effect:

because
so
As a result,
Consequently,
Therefore,

Your experience counts!

Directions: Write about or discuss the following questions.
1. Is anyone in your family a teacher? What about your friends?
2. Do you think you would like to be a teacher? Why or why not? If so, what age would you like to teach?
3. Do you think that teachers are well-paid?
4. What can school districts do to attract more teachers?

Word Search

Directions: Find the words.

A	U	T	H	O	R	I	Z	A	T	I	O	N	A
D	E	D	U	C	T	I	B	L	E	B	F	N	U
N	M	F	O	R	T	U	N	A	T	E	Q	S	W
B	E	X	P	E	N	S	I	V	E	N	O	U	P
T	R	S	H	C	O	N	S	I	D	E	R	R	Q
D	G	W	Y	H	G	A	B	U	Z	F	R	G	A
K	E	A	S	I	C	K	L	I	M	I	T	E	D
W	N	W	I	N	J	U	R	E	D	T	P	R	S
P	C	N	C	O	V	E	R	E	D	S	N	Y	I
W	Y	D	I	J	R	N	W	F	N	F	H	N	I
K	R	P	A	T	I	E	N	T	E	S	M	F	T
W	V	U	N	I	V	E	R	S	A	L	H	E	S
F	C	N	I	Q	N	H	Y	G	R	W	A	Y	S
P	H	I	Z	N	L	Z	P	O	L	I	C	Y	K
H	O	E	A	M	I	U	Z	M	Y	W	U	T	O

authorization expensive   physician
benefits   fortunate   policy
consider   injured   sick
covered   limited   surgery
deductible   nearly   universal
emergency   patient

Lesson 4

Prereading Discussion Questions:

If you need to go to the doctor, who is responsible for the bills?
Does the government provide health care benefits to people in the United
   States? If so, for whom?

Summary:
   Even if you have health insurance, it costs a lot of money to get health care in the United States. Not everything is paid for by insurance, but the really expensive things are. Patients may need to pay for some things, but if they get really sick or need surgery, the insurance will pay for most of it.

   Many people get insurance through the workplace. They are members of a group insurance policy. Everyone in the group has the same benefits. Other people get individual health insurance policies. These people buy their insurance directly from the company.

---

surgery = an operation
benefits = something extra an
   employer gives
universal = for everyone
fortunate = lucky

consider = think about
patient = sick person
authorization = permission
emergency = very serious
   situation; immediate
   attention is necessary

Health Insurance as an Employee Benefit

[1] Health care is very expensive in the United States. Unlike many countries, the US does not have a universal national health care plan, so health insurance is a very important thing to have.

[2] Many employees are fortunate to get health insurance as a benefit. The employees are part of a group insurance policy. This means that everyone in the plan has the same insurance benefits.

[3] People who do not have health insurance benefits at work should consider getting private health insurance. Individual health insurance is expensive, but getting sick is more expensive.

[4] There are several different types of group health insurance. Most are either Health Maintenance Organizations (HMOs), or Preferred Provider Organizations (PPOs).

[5] HMOs pay for more services but the patient is limited in where he or she can go to get these services. The HMO gives a list of doctors and usually one or two hospitals. If the patient uses those doctors and hospitals, insurance pays for nearly everything. If he or she goes to a different doctor or hospital, insurance pays nothing. In addition, it is necessary for the patient to get *preauthorization* before visiting an emergency room, except in life-threatening emergencies.

[6] PPOs give the patient more freedom to choose the physician or hospital, but there is usually a *deductible* or *co-pay*. A deductible is a minimum payment for the year. If your insurance policy has a $100 deductible, the patient must pay the first $100. After that, the insurance begins to pay. A co-pay is an amount (typically 20%) that the patient is responsible for each hospital admission, office visit, or prescription.

[7] Some services are not covered by health insurance, such as eyeglasses or hearing aids. However, health insurance protects people from needing to pay very large hospital bills if they get sick or injured.

Vocabulary in Context

Directions: Find the synonyms in the reading.

Line #	Find a synonym for:	Synonym
4	available for everyone	
8	lucky	
9	something extra which an employer gives	
28	restricted, not everything is allowed	
34	almost	
38	permission in advance	
40	very serious; death is possible	
44	doctor	
45	money the patient must pay before the insurance starts	
52	the part of the charge that the patient must pay	
63	hurt	

Comprehension Check

Directions: Read each sentence and decide if it is true or false.

1. Everyone in the United States has health insurance.
2. Some people get health insurance as a benefit at work.
3. It is not possible for individuals to get health insurance.
4. Health insurance pays for all medical services.
5. People with life-threatening emergencies should go to the emergency room whether or not they have insurance.
6. Health insurance is not very expensive.

Directions: Answer these questions:

7. Why do people need to have insurance?
8. Where is the best place to get insurance? Why?
9. What should people do if they don't get insurance at work? Why don't more people do this?
10. Most insurance policies fall into two categories. What are they?
11. What do the acronyms stand for?
12. What are the advantages of an HMO? What are the disadvantages?
13. What are the advantages of an PPO? What are the disadvantages?
14. What are some examples of things which are often not covered by insurance? Can you think of anything else?

In other words...

Directions: Match the sentences with the same meanings.

___1. The US does not have a national health care plan.

___2. Many employees are fortunate to get health insurance as a benefit.

___3. Everyone in the group has the same insurance benefits.

___4. People who do not get insurance benefits at work should consider getting private health insurance.

___5. The patient is limited in where he or she can go to get services.

___6. If the patient uses these doctors and hospitals, insurance pays for nearly everything.

___7. It is necessary to get preauthorization before visiting the emergency room, except in life-threatening emergencies.

___8. The patient has more freedom to choose the physician or hospital, but there is usually a deductible or co-pay.

___9. The patient pays the first $100. After that, the insurance begins to pay.

___10. Health insurance protects people from needing to pay very large hospital bills if they get sick or injured.

a) Workers are lucky if they get health care as one of their benefits.

b) Private insurance is something that people ought to consider if they don't have insurance at work.

c) There are only specific hospitals and doctors that the patients can go to.

d) Before going to the emergency room, the patient needs to get permission in advance, unless it is a life-or-death situation.

e) There is usually a cost for the patient, but it is possible to choose any doctor or any hospital.

f) Insurance will pay for almost everything if the patient uses only the right physicians and facilities.

g) Insurance starts to pay after the patient has met the $100 deductible.

h) If people become ill or get hurt, medical insurance helps to protect them from very large hospital bills.

i) There is no universal health care program in the US.

j) All the members of the group have the same coverage.

Main Ideas

Directions: Refer to the reading to find the main ideas of these paragraphs:

Paragraphs 1, 2, and 3
    a) Everyone in the plan has the same benefits.
    b) People who do not have health insurance at work should think about getting individual insurance.
    c) Health care in the United States is very expensive, so it's important for people to have medical insurance.

Paragraph 5
    a) HMOs pay for almost everything, but there are restrictions on what doctors and hospitals the patients can go to.
    b) It is necessary to get preauthorization before going to the emergency room.
    c) The HMO gives a list of doctors and hospitals.

Paragraph 6
    a) A deductible is the minimum payment for a year.
    b) PPOs give more flexibility, but they are more expensive for the patient.
    c) A co-pay is an amount that the patient is responsible for when they go to the doctor or hospital.

Synonyms

Directions: Match the words with the same meanings.

____ 1. expensive
____ 2. types
____ 3. covered
____ 4. nearly
____ 5. universal
____ 6. limited
____ 7. policy
____ 8. sick
____ 9. life-threatening
____ 10. injured

a. contract for insurance
b. paid for
c. for everyone
d. ill
e. almost
f. costing a lot of money
g. very serious; death is possible
h. hurt
i. restricted
j. kinds

Suffix –ible/able

The suffix –ible/able means *can, is capable of, or with a particular quality*.
The new word is an adjective.

	Example	Meaning
From the reading:	deductible	can be deducted
	responsible	can respond to; can answer for
Other examples:	manageable	can be managed (done with difficulty)
	comfortable	with the quality of comfort
	reversible	can be reversed (turned inside-out)
	visible	can be seen
	tolerable	can be tolerated
	objectionable	can offend; people can object to it

Directions: Use the examples to complete the sentences. Be sure to use a plural form when necessary. Use each word only once.

1. The seats in my new car are very _____. I can ride for a long time, and my back doesn't hurt.
2. The company was _____ for your injury so you should give the hospital bill to your boss.
3. My new jacket is _____. It is red on one side and blue on the other.
4. It's very cloudy tonight so the moon is not _____.
5. The other driver didn't have insurance, so I had to pay my $500 _____.
6. There are six of us living in a very small apartment. It's not great, but it's _____.
7. Some people don't like to go to the movies because they find bad language _____.
8. It's very hot today. However, I have a fan, so it's _____.

Scanning

Vocabulary:

HMO	hospitalization	covered	short-term
physician	maternity	provided	deductible
chiropractor	physical fitness programs	prevailing fee	co-pay
routine	greater	usual and customary fee	in full

Summary of Insurance Benefits

	Pinnacle Insurance Company (Employee chooses doctor and hospital)	Health Plus HMO (Services must be approved by HMO physician)	Family Care HMO (Services must be approved by HMO physician)
Hospitalization	$100 co-pay	covered in full	provided in full
Medical/Surgical	$25,000 max per illness	covered in full	provided in full
Maternity	usual and customary charges; dependent daughters covered	covered in full; dependent daughters covered	covered in full; dependent daughters covered
X-rays and lab tests	prevailing fee covered in full	covered in full	provided in full
Emergency care	prevailing fee covered in full	covered in full	provided in full
Physician/Chiropractor visits	80%	covered in full	provided in full
Physical Therapy	80%	covered in full	short-term provided in full
Prescription Drugs	$5.00 co-pay	covered in full after $50 deductible; $100 per family maximum	provided in full at Family Care Pharmacy
Mental Health	80%	20 visits or $1800, whichever is greater	covered in full

Directions: Scan the table to find the answers to these questions.

1. In which plan does the patient need to pay for hospitalization?

2. Which plan(s) cover medical and surgical procedures in full?

3. Which plan(s) cover dependent daughters if they get pregnant?

4. If you have insurance with the Pinnacle Insurance Company and you need X-rays, will they pay in full?

5. If you need to go to the doctor and you have Pinnacle Insurance, will you need to pay?

6. If you need emergency room care and you have insurance with the Health Plus HMO, will you need to pay?

7. If you have insurance with the Family Care HMO and you need physical therapy will you have to pay?

Crossword Puzzle

Across
2. very serious situation; immediate attention is necessary
5. lucky
8. permission
9. ill
10. for everyone
14. think about
15. sick person
16. hurt

Down
1. money the patient must pay before the insurance starts
3. costing a lot of money
4. something extra an employer gives
6. operation
7. doctor
11. restricted
12. paid for
13. almost
15. contract for insurance

✏ Get ready to write!

Prepare for writing
Directions: **On a separate piece of paper, outline the article.** Use the main ideas you found in the exercise on p.36 as the headings. Next, add the details that go with the main ideas. Your teacher will help you.

Write a summary
Directions: **Use the outline to help you write 3 paragraphs which summarize the article.** Be sure to:

- use a capital letter at the beginning of each sentence.
- use periods to separate sentences.
- indent to show the beginning of each paragraph.

Tip:
We use the following expressions when we contrast the differences between two or more people or things.

    but
    however
    although
    even though
    on the other hand,…

Your experience counts!

Directions: Write about or discuss the following questions.

1. Why is it good for employers to give their employees insurance? Does it help the company? If so, how?
2. What experiences have you or your family had with hospitals in the US? How do they compare with the hospitals and clinics in other countries?
3. Why is it important to see the doctor regularly, and not just when you are sick?

Word Search

Directions: Find the words.

A	C	C	O	M	M	O	D	A	T	I	O	N	S
P	R	O	D	U	C	T	I	V	I	T	Y	A	I
I	N	E	X	P	E	N	S	I	V	E	O	R	L
F	I	N	E	F	U	N	C	T	I	O	N	A	L
C	D	C	O	N	C	E	R	N	E	D	O	I	E
D	I	S	A	B	I	L	I	T	Y	P	U	S	G
O	M	A	C	C	O	M	M	O	D	A	T	E	A
H	M	P	O	S	I	T	I	O	N	V	R	B	L
E	E	H	E	L	P	U	N	C	T	U	A	L	I
X	D	D	E	C	R	E	A	S	E	Z	E	O	D
P	O	G	T	C	O	S	T	L	Y	Z	Z	C	M
E	M	P	L	O	Y	E	E	S	V	Y	C	K	B
N	H	I	R	E	X	H	D	O	R	U	Y	S	Q
S	P	M	X	X	Q	B	M	P	Q	M	K	Y	B
E	D	X	R	I	T	Q	Z	Y	Q	T	E	C	Y

Accommodate	Discriminate	Inexpensive
Accommodations	Employees	Out
Blocks	Expense	Position
Concerned	Fine	Productivity
Costly	Functional	Punctual
Decrease	Help	Raise
Dimmed	Hire	
Disability	Illegal	

Lesson 5

Prereading Discussion Questions:

What is a *disability*?
Do you know anyone who is disabled? What kind of help do they need?

Summary:

There are many people with disabilities living in the United States. It is sometimes difficult for them to find jobs because they may need special help from the employer. Employers are not supposed to discriminate against the disabled, but sometimes they don't know how to help these workers. They also might be afraid that adapting the job will be expensive. They also worry about decreasing productivity.

Employers often find that very simple, inexpensive changes are all that is necessary to accommodate disabled workers. They may also learn that some of these workers are better employees than the non-disabled workers.

---

to discriminate = to be unfair
disabled = with a physical problem
to adapt = to accommodate; to change for someone with special needs
to accommodate = to adapt; to change for someone with special needs

to decrease = to make less
productivity = the ability to produce work
non-disabled = without a disability

Hiring the Disabled Can Be a Good Deal for Employers

[1] All companies say that they do not discriminate against people with disabilities. They have to say it. The government says discrimination is illegal. Employers must be fair to disabled workers. If they aren't fair, they may have to pay a big fine.

[2] Most companies want to do the right thing, but it isn't always easy to know how to help the disabled in the workplace. Many employers worry that the disabled will be late or absent more than other workers. They also worry that disabled workers will get hurt more often. Companies are also concerned that they won't be able to do the job. This could decrease productivity.

[3] Many employers are surprised to learn that disabled workers take less sick time than other workers. According to Millicent Overland, of Farrimore Technologies, Inc., her disabled workers are actually absent less often than other workers.

[4] "I was concerned that disabled workers would be out more often. We have found that the opposite is true. Our disabled employees work very hard. They are just as productive as the rest of the workforce," Overland said. She expected problems but there weren't any.

[5] Some employers are also concerned about the expense to make the workplace functional for the disabled. They know that they must accommodate the workers' needs, but they don't want to spend a lot of money.

[6] The employers really don't need to worry. Some changes are not very expensive. With these changes, the disabled employees can work just as well as other workers. For example, a worker with sensitive eyes may be able to work in an office if the lights are dimmed. In another example, it is hard for someone in a wheel chair to use a standard desk because it is too low. There is a simple solution. It can be raised on blocks of wood.

[7] Many employers think that it is important to be on time. It causes problems when employees are late. Supervisors are surprised that many disabled workers are very punctual. According to Overland, the disabled workers at her company are rarely late. They have excellent work habits. They are very dependable workers, she says.

Vocabulary in Context

Directions: Find the synonyms in the reading.

Line #	Find a synonym for:	Synonym
2	show prejudice or bias to (2 words)	
3	physical or emotional problems	
5	against the law	
5	honest; equal	
7	money as a penalty	
15	worried	
17	the ability to produce work	
29	equally (2 words)	
34	cost; price	
35	workable	
37	adapt to	
46	made less bright	
50	put up	
55	on time	

Comprehension Check

Directions: Read each sentence and decide if it is <u>true</u> or <u>false</u>.

1. No companies discriminate against the disabled.
2. No companies are supposed to discriminate against the disabled.
3. Employers worry that disabled workers will get hurt.
4. Supervisors worry that disabled workers will be less productive than other workers.
5. Supervisors are not concerned about workers who are absent.
6. All changes to the workplace cost a lot of money.
7. People in wheelchairs can't sit at standard desks.

Directions: Answer these questions:

8. Why do companies say they don't discriminate against workers with disabilities? Is it true?
9. What are some of the concerns of the employers?
10. Was Millicent Overland concerned? What did she learn?
11. What are some simple accommodations that companies can make to help their disabled employees?
12. What happens to employers who do not follow the law? Is this right? Are there similar laws in other countries?

In other words…

Directions: Match the sentences with the same meanings.

___1. Companies say that they do not discriminate against disabled people.

___2. Employers who are unfair to disabled workers may have to pay a big fine.

___3. It isn't always easy to find ways to help people with disabilities in the workplace.

___4. They are concerned that productivity will decrease.

___5. Disabled workers take less sick time than other workers.

___6. Some employers are concerned about the expense to make the workplace functional for the disabled.

___7. Employers know that they must accommodate the worker's needs.

___8. With changes, disabled workers can work as well as other employees.

___9. Many companies can accommodate disabled workers with inexpensive changes.

___10. Someone in a wheelchair can use a standard desk if it is raised on blocks of wood.

a) Disabled employees are out sick less frequently.

b) It may be expensive to modify the workplace to meet the needs of the disabled and this worries the employers.

c) Modifications that don't cost a lot of money can help disabled workers in many companies.

d) Workers who use wheelchairs can use the same desks as everyone else, if they are put up on pieces of wood.

e) Disabled people are treated fairly, according to companies.

f) Companies are aware that they need to adapt to the disability of the worker.

g) It's sometimes hard to know how to help the disabled at work.

h) With accommodation, disabled and non-disabled employees can work equally well.

i) Employers worry that disabled workers will not be as productive.

j) Companies who discriminate may have to pay a price.

Main Ideas

Directions: Refer to the reading to find the main ideas of these paragraphs:

Paragraph 1
    a) Many employers worry about disabled workers.
    b) It is against the law to discriminate against people with disabilities.
    c) Companies who are unfair must pay fines.

Paragraph 2
    a) Many employers are afraid to hire the disabled.
    b) They want to do the right thing.
    c) Workers may become less productive.

Paragraph 7
    a) Disabled workers are less punctual.
    b) Employers are sometimes surprised to learn that the disabled may be better workers than non-disabled employees.
    c) It causes problems when employees are late.

Synonyms

Directions: Match the words with same meanings.

_____ 1. fine (n.)   a. expensive
_____ 2. punctual   b. worried
_____ 3. blocks   c. against the law
_____ 4. costly   d. out
_____ 5. accommodate   e. on time
_____ 6. concerned   f. put up
_____ 7. illegal   g. penalty
_____ 8. absent   h. square pieces
_____ 9. raise (v.)   i. lowered
_____ 10. dimmed   j. adapt to

Suffix –ity

The suffix –ity makes the word a *noun with a specific characteristic*.

	Example	Meaning
From the reading:	disability	characteristic: disabled
	productivity	characteristic: productive; producing well
Other examples:	stupidity	characteristic: stupid
	regularity	characteristic: regular
	flexibility	characteristic: flexible
	curiosity	characteristic: curious
	novelty	characteristic: new; novel
	ability	characteristic: able to do something
	quantity	characteristic: number; amount

Directions: Use the examples to complete the sentences. Use each word only once.

1. The boss asked Elroy about the _____ of material in the storeroom.
2. Cellular phones were a _____ in the 1980's.
3. Employers must make accommodation if their employee has a _____.
4. The teachers can change a student's school schedule if his or her work schedule changes. The students are happy about the _____ of the program.
5. Children love to ask questions. They have a natural _____.
6. Many people were absent during the flu epidemic and the manager was concerned about a decrease in _____.
7. An excellent sense of rhythm is the reason that Michael has the _____ to dance so well.
8. I often see Julie at the library because she studies with _____.

Scanning

Essential and Non-essential functions

Certain skills and abilities are necessary for every job. Employers need to decide which skills are essential for the job so disabled people will know which jobs are appropriate for them.

This table shows examples of these abilities and how they are used in specific jobs.

Category of job	Occupation	Seeing	Reading and Writing	Talking and Hearing	Standing and Walking
Hospitality	Cashier	ESSENTIAL	ESSENTIAL	ESSENTIAL	NON-ESSENTIAL
	Dishwasher	ESSENTIAL*	NON-ESSENTIAL	NON-ESSENTIAL	ESSENTIAL
	Housekeeping	ESSENTIAL	NON-ESSENTIAL	NON-ESSENTIAL	ESSENTIAL
Factory	Machine operator	ESSENTIAL	NON-ESSENTIAL	NON-ESSENTIAL	NON-ESSENTIAL
	Quality Control	ESSENTIAL	ESSENTIAL	ESSENTIAL	NON-ESSENTIAL
Office	Clerk/Typist	ESSENTIAL*	ESSENTIAL	NON-ESSENTIAL	NON-ESSENTIAL
	Accountant	ESSENTIAL	ESSENTIAL	ESSENTIAL	NON-ESSENTIAL
	Computer Operator	ESSENTIAL*	ESSENTIAL	ESSENTIAL	NON-ESSENTIAL
Mechanical repair	Bicycle repair	ESSENTIAL	NON-ESSENTIAL	NON-ESSENTIAL	NON-ESSENTIAL
	Small engine repair	ESSENTIAL	ESSENTIAL	NON-ESSENTIAL	NON-ESSENTIAL
Health Care	Dietary Aide	ESSENTIAL	NON-ESSENTIAL	NON-ESSENTIAL	ESSENTIAL
	Laundry Aide	ESSENTIAL	NON-ESSENTIAL	NON-ESSENTIAL	ESSENTIAL

*can be done by a blind person with accommodation

Directions: Scan the table to find the answers to the following questions.

1. If you are visually-impaired (blind), what are some of the jobs you can do? What kinds of accommodations would be necessary?
2. What are considered essential functions for the job of accountant?
3. Some people with learning disabilities are unable to read. Which jobs would be appropriate for them?
4. For which jobs are hearing and speaking not essential? Why? How do deaf people in these jobs communicate with their hearing co-workers?
5. Not all jobs require the ability to speak. Which are they?
6. If you like to work with your hands and you are hearing-impaired (deaf), which jobs would be good?

Crossword Puzzle

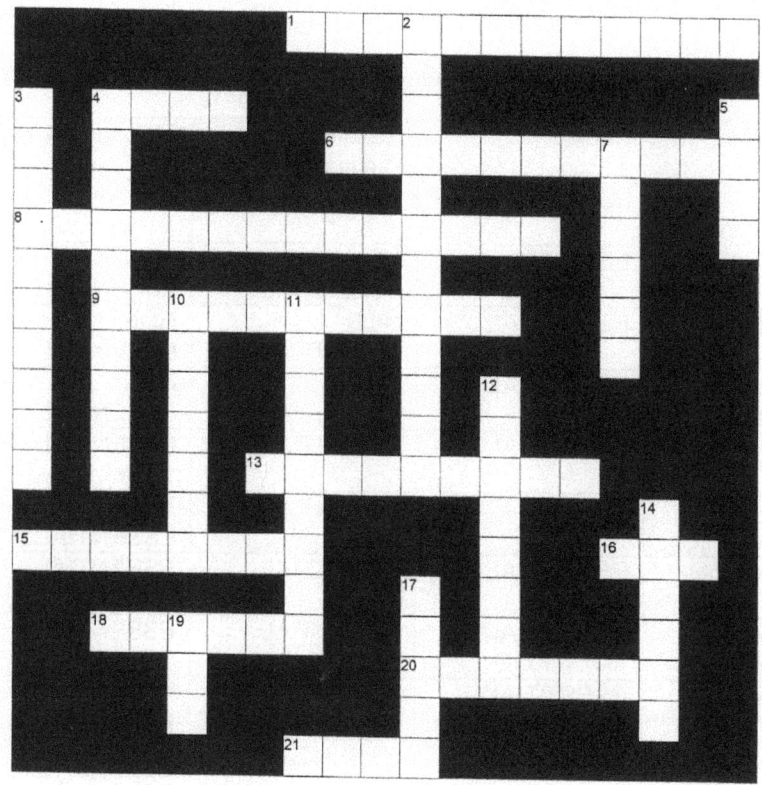

Across
1. the ability to produce work
4. money you must pay as a penalty
6. adapt to someone's needs
8. changes to meet special needs
9. for not a lot of money
13. worried
15. become less
16. position
18. square pieces
20. against the law
21. give a job to

Down
2. treat unfairly
3. physical, mental, or learning problem
4. workable; usable
5. assistance
7. made darker
10. cost; price
11. workers
12. on time
14. expensive
17. put up
19. absent

✏ Get ready to write!

Prepare for writing
Directions: **On a separate piece of paper, outline the article.** Use the main ideas you found in the exercise on p.46 as the headings. Next, add the details that go with the main ideas. Your teacher will help you.

Write a summary
Directions: **Use the outline to help you write 3 paragraphs which summarize the article.** Be sure to:
- use a capital letter at the beginning of each sentence.
- use periods to separate sentences.
- indent to show the beginning of each paragraph.

Tip:
Sometimes we want to argue that something is not true. We can use the bold-faced expressions to do that.

Many people think that all fat is unhealthy.	On the contrary,	some oils, like olive oil, are good for you.
	To the contrary,	
	Nothing can be further from the truth.	Some oils, like olive oil, are good for you.
	This is absolutely untrue.	
	This is categorically untrue.	
	This is not at all true.	

Your experience counts!

Directions: Write about or discuss the following questions.
1. Do you know anyone who is disabled? Did he/she have trouble finding a job? Why?
2. Think of an example when non-disabled people need to interact with disabled workers. Is it hard? How can they communicate?

Word Search

Directions: Find the words.

U	N	F	O	R	T	U	N	A	T	E	L	Y	A	A
C	O	N	T	R	I	B	U	T	E	L	N	A	G	E
A	V	O	L	U	N	T	E	E	R	E	T	I	R	E
L	G	Z	N	D	E	P	O	S	I	T	A	X	O	J
C	W	I	T	H	D	R	A	W	X	E	L	M	W	M
U	U	E	P	S	C	E	N	N	K	N	N	O	J	T
L	F	Z	E	I	G	P	E	A	M	O	U	N	T	V
A	O	N	N	C	T	A	C	C	O	U	N	T	A	X
T	R	M	A	J	O	R	Z	Z	S	G	B	H	F	N
E	M	P	L	O	Y	E	E	J	P	H	R	L	R	Y
L	U	J	T	I	C	D	L	L	G	G	W	Y	D	M
T	L	N	Y	Q	E	A	X	H	R	T	V	J	U	F
J	A	E	M	N	L	W	D	M	M	J	H	S	F	C

Account
Age
Amount
Calculate
Contribute
Deposit
Employee

Enough
Formula
Grow
Major
Monthly
Penalty
Prepared

Retire
Tax
Unfortunately
Volunteer
Withdraw

Lesson 6

Prereading Discussion Questions:

What is retirement?
When do people retire? Why do people retire?

What are the pros of being retired? What are the cons?
Where do people get money to live on when they are retired?

Summary:

People generally retire at approximately age 65. Because they no longer work, they don't get a paycheck from a company anymore. Most people rely on Social Security income, which is like a government pension. It only pays for approximately half of a person's living expenses, leaving the retired person with a problem.

Some people save money and invest it while they are still working. The money that they put in their retirement account when they are in their 20's, 30's, 40's, and 50's will give them a monthly check when they retire, in addition to Social Security. This extra money will make their retirement much more comfortable.

---

pension = retirement income

rely on = depend on

expenses = money going out of a family, like rent, electricity, food, etc.

invest = to put money somewhere (a company or a bank) where it will (hopefully!) grow larger

monthly = every month

401(k) = an investment plan for retirement; available only through an employer

Retirement Benefits Make Old Age Easier

[1] Most workers in the United States get a monthly Social Security check when they retire. Unfortunately, a Social Security check isn't large enough to take care of all of a retired person's expenses.

[2] It is important for people to remember to plan for their own retirement. They need to save money from every paycheck and put it into a retirement account.

[3] People who have a retirement account separate from Social Security will have a much more comfortable retirement because they will get two checks every month. One will be from Social Security, and the other will be from their retirement account.

[4] There are two main types of retirement accounts. The first is a *defined benefit plan*, which the employer provides. The second type is the responsibility of the worker. It is called a *defined contribution plan*.

[5] Defined benefit plans are paid for by the employer. They promise you a specific amount of money every month after retirement. In many cases the plan uses a formula with information about your salary when you were working, your age and the number of years of service on the job to calculate your monthly benefit.

[6] Defined contribution plans work differently. The employee deposits money from each paycheck into the account. The employer may or may not also contribute money. The money grows over the years, and at retirement, the worker receives the amount that is in the account. 401 (k) and an Individual Retirement Account (IRA) are typical defined contribution accounts. The major difference between the two accounts is that a 401(k) is from an employer and an IRA is a bank account.

[7] Putting money into one of these accounts means that you will pay less in taxes. Money you put away for retirement isn't taxed until you take it out of the account. If you wait until after you retire, you will pay lower taxes because your income will be lower. If you withdraw it before you retire, you will have to pay the taxes and a penalty.

[8] People who plan for retirement are usually better prepared. They can enjoy their "golden years". They can travel, spend time with their grandchildren, or volunteer in their community. They may not be rich, but they won't have to worry about money all the time, either.

Vocabulary in Context

Directions: Find the synonyms in the reading.

Line #	Find a synonym for:	Synonym
2	every month	
4	stop working due to age	
4	it's too bad that…..	
8	money you need to pay	
14	a record of money going in and coming out	
30	something which is given, like money, help, or ideas	
37	a mathematical rule	
41	use math to find the answer	
49	gets bigger	
56	very important	
68	money coming into a family	
69	take out	
71	money you pay because you did something bad	

Comprehension Check

Directions: Read each sentence and decide if it is <u>true</u> or <u>false</u>.

1. Everybody in the US gets Social Security when they retire.
2. People who live on Social Security alone live comfortably.
3. Workers need to save money for their own retirement.
4. You never have to pay tax on the money in your 401(k) account.
5. Retirement will be much more comfortable for people who have a second income.
6. Retired people can use the extra money for travel or for their families.

Directions: Answer these questions:

7. How often do retired people get a Social Security check?
8. Are these checks enough to live comfortably?
9. What can workers do to make sure that their retirement will be more comfortable?
10. What are some different types of retirement plans?
11. How is a defined benefit plan different from a defined contribution plan?
12. How is a 401(k) different from an IRA?
13. How does putting money in a retirement account help people when they are young?
14. If you need to take money out of your retirement account before you retire, what will happen?

In other words...

Directions: Match the sentences with the same meanings.

___1. Most workers in the United States get a monthly Social Security check when they retire.

___2. A Social Security check isn't large enough to take care of all of a retired person's expenses.

___3. People who have a retirement account separate from Social Security will have a much more comfortable retirement.

___4. Defined benefit plans are paid for by the employer.

___5. Defined contribution accounts are the responsibility of the worker.

___6. The retirement plan may use a formula to calculate your monthly benefit.

___7. A 401(k) account is from an employer.

___8. An IRA is from a bank.

___9. Money you put away for retirement isn't taxed until you take it out of the account.

___10. If you withdraw it before you retire, you will have to pay the taxes and a penalty.

a) Retirement will be much easier for people who have a separate retirement account.

b) Employees are responsible for putting money into defined contribution plans.

c) Some plans may use a mathematical rule to figure out how large your monthly check will be.

d) The money from Social Security isn't sufficient to pay for everything a person needs.

e) An employer provides a 401(k) account.

f) If an employee wants an IRA, he or she must go to a bank.

g) In addition to taxes, there is an extra charge if you take the money out of the account before you retire.

h) Most US workers get a check every month from Social Security.

i) You don't pay tax on the money until you withdraw it from the account.

j) The employer pays for defined benefit accounts.

Main Ideas

Directions: Refer to the reading to find the main ideas of these paragraphs:

Paragraph 1, 2, and 3
    a) A Social Security check isn't very big.
    b) Some people get two checks every month.
    c) Workers need to plan for their own retirement.

Paragraph 4
    a) There are two main types of retirement accounts.
    b) The employer puts money into the retirement account.
    c) The worker puts money into the retirement account.

Paragraph 7
    a) The employer may contribute to the retirement account.
    b) There are tax benefits for putting money in a retirement account.
    c) A penalty is required.

Opposites

Directions: Match the words with the opposite meanings.

____ 1. income   a. get paid

____ 2. grows   b. bonus

____ 3. major   c. employee

____ 4. penalty   d. insufficient

____ 5. volunteer   e. in the same way

____ 6. difference   f. expenses

____ 7. employer   g. shrinks

____ 8. enough   h. similarity

____ 9. differently   i. more

____ 10. less   j. minor; unimportant

Suffix –*ment*

The suffix –*ment* changes a verb into a noun.

	Verb	Noun
From the reading:	retire	retirement
Other examples:	develop	development
	disappoint	disappointment
	govern	government
	arrange	arrangement
	manage	management
	measure	measurement
	refresh	refreshment

Directions: Use the examples to complete the sentences. Be sure to use the plural form when necessary.

1. Accurate _____ is important if you work in construction.

2. John just got promoted to _____. He's my boss now.

3. You can buy _____ in the cafeteria.

4. It is important for a teacher to know about the _____ of children.

5. What is the _____ for the party tonight?

6. _____ usually happens when a person is over sixty.

7. When I told her that I couldn't go, I saw the _____ in her eyes.

8. Senators and Representatives are members of the federal _____.

Scanning

Directions: Scan the example* in the table to find the answers to the following questions.

Paycheck without 401(k) deduction		Paycheck with 401(k) deduction		401(k) plan	
$480	gross taxable income	$480	gross pay	$50	Employee contribution
		-50	401(k) contribution	$50	Matching funds (from company)
		430	taxable income		
-60	federal tax	-50	federal tax		
420	subtotal	380	subtotal		
-20	state tax	-15	state tax		
400	subtotal	365	subtotal		
-20	FICA (Social Security tax)	-15	FICA (Social Security tax)		
380	subtotal	350	subtotal		
-15	Medicare tax	-10	Medicare tax		
$365	net take home pay	$340	net take home pay	$100	Total contribution

1. In the above example, how much does the employee contribute to the company's 401(k) plan?
2. What is the difference in the take home pay of the employee with and without a contribution to a 401(k) plan?
3. How much does the employee pay in Federal tax if he/she doesn't put money into the company's 401(k) plan? How much does he/she pay with a contribution?
4. The third column shows matching funds. What does this mean? Why is this good for the employee?
5. The third column shows a $100 total contribution. How much does the employee really pay to put $100 in his or her account? Where does the rest of the money come from?

---

* example is <u>completely</u> hypothetical

Crossword Puzzle

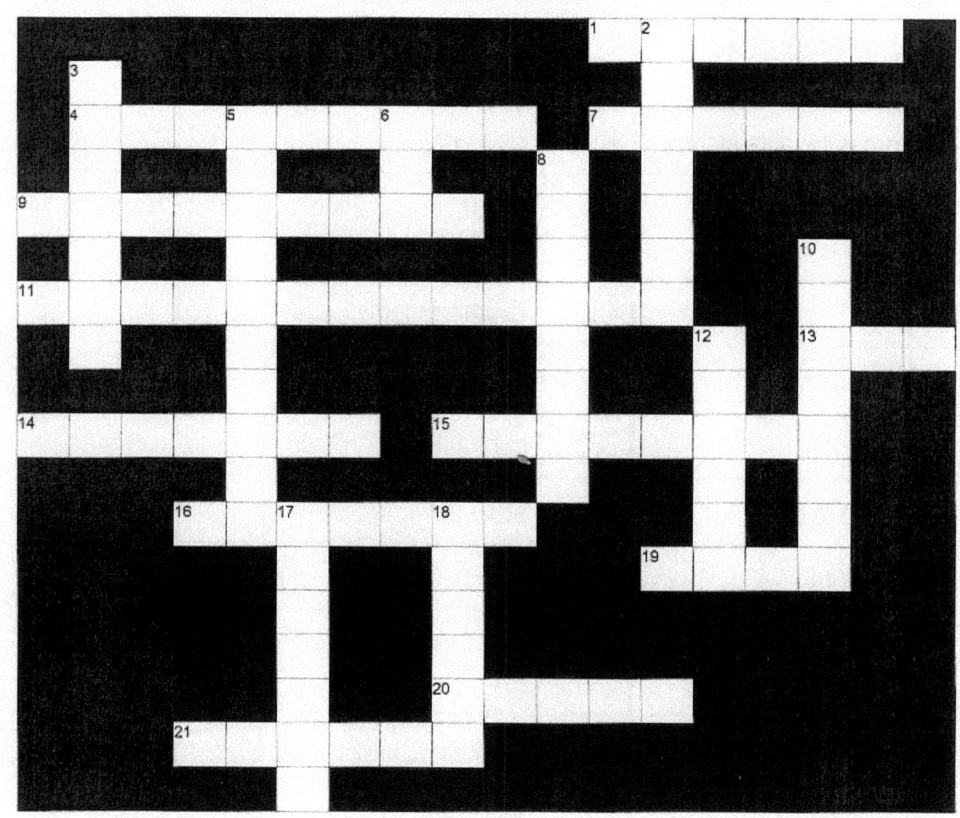

Across
1. how much
4. figure out with math
7. sufficient
9. work with no pay
11. It's too bad….
13. money you pay to the government
14. a mathematical rule
15. ready
16. put in
19. get bigger
20. very important
21. stop working due to age

Down
2. once a month
3. a record of money, in a bank, for example
5. give money, help, or ideas
6. how old
8. money going out
10. take out
12. employee
17. money you pay because you did something wrong
18. money coming in

✏ Get ready to write!

Prepare for writing
Directions: On a separate piece of paper, outline the article. Use the main ideas you found in the exercise on p.56 as the headings. Next, add the details that go with the main ideas. Your teacher will help you.

Write a summary
Directions: Use the outline to help you write 3 paragraphs which summarize the article. Be sure to:
- use a capital letter at the beginning of each sentence.
- use periods to separate sentences.
- indent to show the beginning of each paragraph.

Tip:
We use the following expressions when we want to give **additional information that agrees with the main idea and makes it stronger**.

and	Students need to study **and** attend class.
also	Students need to study. They **also** need to attend class.
as well	Students need to study. They need to attend class **as well**.
furthermore	Students need to study. **Furthermore,** they need to attend class.
moreover	Students need to study. **Moreover,** they need to attend class.
in addition	Students need to study. **In addition,** they need to attend class.
as well as	Students need to study **as well as** attend class.

Your experience counts!

Directions: Write about or discuss the following questions.

1. Think about the retired people you know. Where do they live? Do they live comfortably?

2. How many years are you from retirement? What do you think you will do?

3. Do people in other countries prepare for retirement? If so, how?

Word Search

Directions: Find the words.

C	A	R	E	G	I	V	E	R	A	G	A	L	O	Z
O	U	T	G	O	I	N	G	B	O	E	T	J	U	D
N	S	C	O	M	F	O	R	T	A	B	L	E	T	Q
C	E	Q	U	I	P	M	E	N	T	B	O	G	L	Y
E	L	E	C	T	R	I	C	A	L	L	O	W	E	D
N	E	N	P	C	O	N	C	E	R	N	E	D	T	L
T	C	O	U	T	D	O	O	R	W	J	T	N	Y	E
R	T	S	I	T	U	A	T	I	O	N	R	M	Q	E
A	R	I	S	G	C	I	T	H	R	I	V	E	I	S
T	P	H	S	I	T	E	X	E	R	C	V	G	Y	K
E	Q	H	U	P	I	P	U	J	I	B	E	Z	Q	G
W	G	S	E	K	V	J	T	Z	E	E	U	X	F	W
A	X	C	Z	R	E	G	A	R	D	L	E	S	S	G

Allowed
Caregiver
Comfortable
Concentrate
Concerned
Electrical

Equipment
Issue
Outdoor
Outgoing
Outlet
Productive

Regardless
Select
Site
Situation
Thrive
Worried

Lesson 7

Prereading Discussion Questions:

Why do families need to find child care for their young children?
How do they find it?

How do they know if they have the right child care for their children?

Summary:

Finding someone to take care of their children is a problem for working parents. They need to know that their children are happy and thriving before they can be productive workers.

It's important for the parents to find the kind of child care which is right for their family. Regardless of the type of care, the site must be clean and safe. Communication with the parents is important for the children to be happy and well cared for.

---

thrive = grow well, develop well
productive = doing a lot of good work
regardless = it doesn't matter; no matter
site = location
issue = problem

caregiver = someone who gives care; teacher
equipment = things you need for a particular activity
electrical outlets = places on the wall to connect to electricity
at ease = comfortable

Who Will Take Care of the Children?

[1] Child care is an important issue for working parents. It is difficult for employees to concentrate on their work and do a good job when they are worried about their children. For this reason, some employers have on-site child care centers.

[2] It is important to choose the right type of daycare. Some families decide to have a family member or friend take care of the children while the parents work. Other families choose a home or commercial day care center for their children.

[3] Communication is the key to a successful day care experience, regardless of what type of day care you choose. It's important to tell the caregiver if your child is shy or outgoing, or whether he or she needs to nap at a certain time. He or she also needs to know if your child has a favorite toy or blanket. At the end of the day, the caregiver needs to give you a full report of your child's activities during the day.

[4] The site must be safe for children. Outdoor play equipment must be in good condition, with soft material underneath. Electrical outlets must be covered and children should not be allowed to play on or near stairs. There also need to be smoke alarms.

[5] It is important to be able to visit your child during the day if you want to. It makes the children happy if their parents visit, and it puts the parent at ease. If the day care provider doesn't want you to visit, find someplace else to take your child.

[6] It is also important to consider the number of children that each adult will have to watch. If there are too many children, they will not get the attention they need.

[7] It isn't always easy to find quality child care, but when parents are careful to ask the right questions, they can usually find a situation that will help their child thrive.

Vocabulary in Context

Directions: Find the synonyms in the reading.

Line #	Find a synonym for:	Synonym
4	think very hard	
7	at the work location	
9	select	
15	business	
19	it doesn't matter	
27	someone who gives care; teacher	
33	things needed for an activity	
35	below	
35	locations to connect to electricity (2 words)	
37	permitted; given permission	
44	comfortable (2 words)	
46	another place (2 words)	
55	good	
58	circumstance; the state of what's happening	
59	grow well	

Comprehension Check

Directions: Read each sentence and decide if it is <u>true</u> or <u>false</u>.

1. Many parents worry about their children during the day.
2. All employers have on-site day care centers.
3. A daily report for the parents is important.
4. Electrical outlets must not be covered.
5. Parents should not visit their children during the day.
6. There need to be smoke alarms.

Directions: Answer these questions:

7. Is it difficult to find good child care?
8. Why is it helpful for an employer to have on-site child care?
9. What three types of day care situations does the article list?
10. Why is communication between parent and teacher so important? What kinds of things must be communicated? What will happen without this communication?
11. What safety precautions does the article suggest? Why are they important? Without them, what will happen?
12. Why should you be worried if the caregiver won't let parents visit?
13. Why is the child/adult ratio important?
14. If you had a child who needed care, where would you take them? Why?

In other words...

Directions: Match the sentences with the same meanings.

___1. Child care is an important issue for working parents.

___2. It is difficult for employees to concentrate on their work when they are worried about their children.

___3. Some employers have on-site child care centers.

___4. It is important to choose the right type of day care.

___5. Communication is the key to a successful day care experience, regardless of what type of day care you choose.

___6. The caregiver needs to give you a full report of your child's activities during the day.

___7. The site must be safe for children.

___8. It makes the children happy if their parents visit, and it puts the parents at ease.

___9. It is important to consider the number of children that each adult will have to watch.

___10. Parents can usually find a situation that will help their child thrive.

a) Choosing appropriate child care is essential.

b) It is important for parents to get a complete report at the end of every day.

c) No matter what kind of day care, communication between parents and caregivers is vital.

d) Visits are good for the children and make the parents feel comfortable.

e) The adult/child ratio is an important consideration.

f) It is usually possible for parents to find circumstances which will help their children develop well.

g) It is important for parents who work to find good care for their children.

h) It is crucial that the location is safe for children.

i) Some companies offer child care for their employees' children in the workplace.

j) When parents are concerned about their children, it's hard for them to be productive workers.

Main Ideas

Directions: Refer to the reading to find the main ideas of these paragraphs:

Paragraph 1
    a) Some employers give their workers time off.
    b) If parents are worried about their children, it is difficult for them to do a good job.
    c) Parents worry about their children.

Paragraph 2
    a) Some parents choose a home day care center.
    b) Commercial day care centers are popular.
    c) Choosing the type of day care which is right for each family is important.

Paragraphs 3, 4, 5, and 6
    a) There are several things to consider when deciding who will take care of the children.
    b) Communication is very important.
    c) Outdoor play equipment must be safe.

Synonyms

Directions: Match the words with the same meanings.

____1. issue   a. grow well

____2. thrive   b. location

____3. needs to   c. not inside

____4. site   d. permitted

____5. outdoor   e. close to

____6. underneath   f. comfortable

____7. allowed   g. problem

____8. near   h. must

____9. at ease   i. think about

____10. consider   j. below

Suffix -ion

The suffix –ion changes a verb into a noun. It means *the act, state, or result of doing something.*

	Verb	Verb + -ion
From the reading:	communicate	communication
	consider	consideration
Other examples:	combine	combination
	complete	completion
	elect	election
	educate	education
	connect	connection
	explain	explanation*
	examine	examination
	investigate	investigation

*note irregular spelling!

Directions: Use the examples to complete the sentences.

1. Because we had a bad _____, I had trouble understanding my friend on the telephone yesterday.
2. US citizens have the right to vote on _____ day.
3. It is necessary to take a written _____ before getting a driver's license.
4. Upon _____ of the written test, a road test is necessary.
5. I don't understand what happened. Please give me an _____.
6. After careful _____, I have decided not to take the new job.
7. The police still don't know what caused the accident so the _____ continues.
8. The _____ of drinking and driving causes many auto accidents.
9. In some states, children must continue their _____ until the age of 18 or until they graduate from high school.
10. E-mail is a modern form of _____.

Scanning

Directions: Scan the table to find the answers to the questions about numbers in licensed Group Childcare Centers with nine or more children.

How many teachers? How many children?[*]

Age of Children	Staff/Child Ratio	Maximum Group Size
Birth to 2	1:4	8
2 to 2.5	1:6	12
2.5-3	1:8	16
3-4	1:10	20
4-5	1:13	24
5-6	1:17	32
6 and older	1:18	32

1. How many teachers must there be if there are 6 infants in a room?
2. Can there be 9 infants in a room if there are 3 teachers?
3. If your son is 2 years and 8 months old, what is the proper staff/child ratio for his classroom?
4. If a child is 3 years old, what is the largest group he/she may be in? How many teachers will there be?
5. How many adults must be present if there are 19 five-year-old children in a classroom?
6. If the group of children is of different ages, what ratio must the center use? Why do you think this is the case?

---

[*]According to the State of Wisconsin Department of Workforce Development pamphlet DES-11065-P (N. 6/98)

Crossword Puzzle

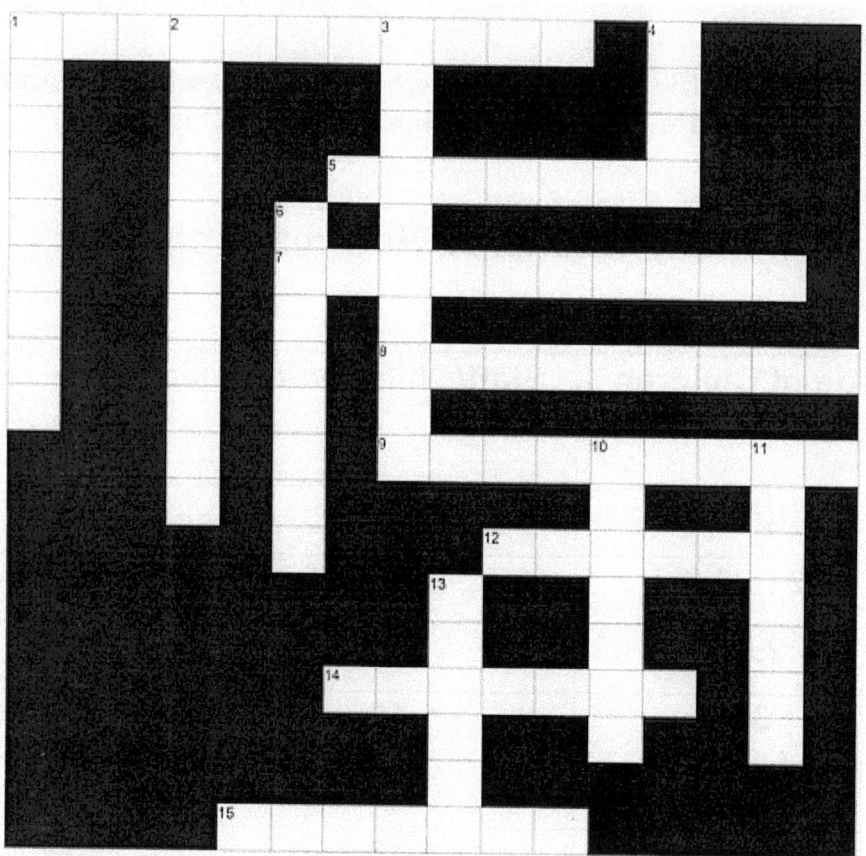

Across

1. think hard
5. a safe place for children to go while their parents are working
7. below
8. things which are necessary for an activity or sport
9. the state of what's happening
12. choose
14. concerned
15. locations to connect to electricity

Down

1. one who gives care; a teacher
2. at ease
3. it doesn't matter; no matter
4. location
6. not shy
10. permitted
11. not in a building; in the fresh air
13. do well; grow well

✏ Get ready to write!

Prepare for writing
Directions: **On a separate piece of paper, outline the article.** Use the main ideas you found in the exercise on p.66 as the headings. Next, add the details that go with the main ideas. Your teacher will help you.

Write a summary
Directions: **Use the outline to help you write 3 paragraphs which summarize the article.** Be sure to:
- use a capital letter at the beginning of each sentence.
- use periods to separate sentences.
- indent to show the beginning of each paragraph.

Tip:
In the affirmative, **must** and **have to** mean the same thing. However, the negative **must not** and **don't have to** have different meanings.

Example:	Meaning:
Workers **must** be on time for work.	It is necessary for workers to be on time for work.
Workers **have to** be on time for work.	
Workers **must not** use drugs or alcohol on the job.	It is forbidden for workers to use drugs or alcohol on the job.
Workers **don't have to** know how to use a computer.	It's OK for workers to know how to use a computer, but it is not necessary.

Your experience counts!

Directions: Write about or discuss the following questions.

1. If you have children, have you ever left them with a babysitter or put them in child care while you went to work? Was it a positive experience for you? Was it a positive experience for your child?

2. As a child, did you go to a babysitter or child care program while your parents worked? Did you like it? Was it good for you?

www.ingramcontent.com/pod-product-compliance
Ingram Content Group UK Ltd.
Pitfield, Milton Keynes, MK11 3LW, UK
UKHW051303180426
11947UKWH00020B/1884